Sunflowers in The Cemetery

Jordyan Richardson

BookLeaf Publishing

India | USA | UK

Presentation by *BookLeaf Publishing*

Web: www.bookleafpub.com

E-mail: info@bookleafpub.com

ISBN: 9789358314915

First edition 2024

To anyone that has ever broken my heart and in such, given me the opportunity to expand my capacity for love and creativity.

And a little bit of "fuck you" sprinkled in.

Recycled Entropy

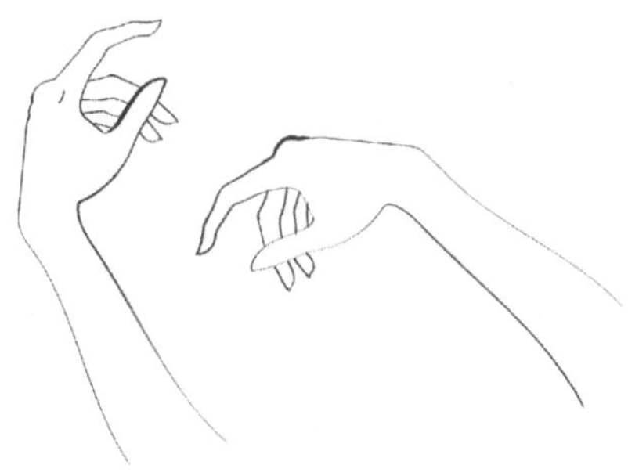

Vini vidi Da Vinci?
I came
I saw
I expressed?
I digress
I confess
I... am depressed
I...cryptic depictions and
I... esoteric descriptions and
I... infinite cerebral relayings and
I... self proclaimed write-ress whom hasn't
written many many moons pass
what sense?
Since always and always since
to process all extrinsic and intrinsic data in
iambic pentameter and verse
To acquiesce that this scarred, glorious
corporeality

This beautiful, sensitive body as it's truth- my
hearse
Transporting all that I...
am?
From blasphemous womb
to isolationism and tomb
To actualize meaning and self
For the sake alone of actualizing meaning and
self.
I, tears of solace for Platonic beauty and
rainbows over the Caribbean and
I, tears of agonizing lamentation for my planet's
pain and..... the pain of my own
all the same
Such heaviness
thousands of pounds bearing down on my
shoulders
.....or just the body weight of all of those leaning
on me
Like every atom of my body 1,2,3...7 billion
times 3
arithmetic etched into my skin designated to
someone's needs or someone counting on me
No mistake however,
I...do not dissent
These bones composed of titanium and
chromium
These tears the sole hydration for black roses
and sunflowers of my soul

This blood of iron from the hearts of dying stars
the stars of dying hearts
and well crafted wordplay
inhale carcinogenic waste of 8 billion heartaches
and a dying planet
exhale dahlias and poetry
Smoke and black mirrors

and maybe...

I... am queen of the underworld where the
universe disposes its dead and decaying
its hopeless notions and shattered dreams
to reanimate to inspire or to catalyze
decomposition for
re-creation
I...live to live amongst the hollowed corpses of
trepidation with-in and with-out
to give
and to construct
Whatever they'll take or become

Naked Daisies

I recognized them
all of them
the girls clad in flesh
inexorably begging for monetary confidence
dazed and nude imploring banknotes to feed
their expenses,
their children,
their addictions.
all of them seeking something-- from me they
wanted to be seen.
greedy seeds rooted in capitalism fertilized by
self-servitude
grew into bear existence
crying
begging

for attention from the sun, but there's nothing to
see when everything is seen
they were daisies without petals
I am the cumulus; I weep for them.

Isolationist

Perchance I should remember myself.
Remember that I haven't brushed my hair in 5
days
and that I can only tell my truth in mazes of
words and verses
and maybe I should remember that I love people
though loathe what some do and the sunsets
though I'm a nyctophobic
and how can a logophile have so little to say?
I wouldn't know.
I have a lot to say though no one to listen.

Early Morning Ramblings

in the ethereal silence found moments before
two mouths discover each other
timelessness is actualized.
The only transient truth
when no other truths are true...
when reality is deliquesce
where there is only two bodies enshrined in
euphoria
likely the few of the only uncountable seconds
in which the world's agony, wars, famines,
dysphoria...
ceases to exist.
big bang birthed upon embrace...
labored, shaky breath sighs
permeate Southern California night skies.
Blowing steadfastly as Santa Ana winds and

gentle 1 a.m Huntington Beach
breezes--caressing our very faces...
the only two faces that matter in a place like
that.

Right?

Like how 2 a.m conducts moonlight requisition
of all of our senses and sense.
Like how 3 a.m manifests some new religion.
Where my body is the temple he worships
inside.
Where my body is the alter he sacrifices himself
at.
Where 6 a.m sun rises to surely promise we find
ourselves back to 1 a.m heaven sometime.

100 Thousand Words

It's reasonable to assume that most people
discover a sense of ease and comfort enveloped
in their cobalt blue cocoon,
not oft I
suffocating and stagnating in the velvet purple
blue roof of this planet.
Let me fly.
I want to be so high I could catch a star
so tired of the rain falling gently on the ground.
so overwhelmed by the walking brain dead.
All suffering collective parataxis distortion.
Why are we ignoring the sunsets and the
refugees?
Why are we ignoring the homeless man,
mentally contorted flashbacks and no food?
Is this the tax paid in our self proclaimed free
world?

Why are we not painting deafening silence with music or watering the daisies with our tears?
Why do the ones lucky enough to be bestowed love so often reject it?
maybe these seemingly incessant inquiries are the true suffocaters. Maybe it's not the sky after all.
Regardless I still long to smell the cosmos and feel him upon my face.
To live and love in earnest even if it is all in vain.
You've asked me what we should eat, I can just eat my words. I have 100 thousand.

Edifying Eden

and my gentle fingertips formed the key to the
gates of a secret garden..
a garden sworn upon to be damned unless chaste
until bought by the highest bidder
a garden spoken as an evil place beguiling
depraved men- to pillage and plunder
a garden that belongs to only me
a garden of good and evil
a garden that bears the fruit of life

a garden, once inside, I realized how
immaculately wondrous this place is-- after, of
course, the ablution of skeletons and bad
intentions..

and inside of her flows nourishing rivers of milk
and honey
when I found the delicate petals of a supple rose
and bestowed upon her my desire to love her and
grow her- transportation to reclamation ensued..
noise subdued, blending into incoherent white
noise
and i was submerged under weight of
indescribable ecstasy-- divine feminine.
and I realized, my garden is a perfect reflection
of every goddess ever dreamt up or imagined.
and a goddess doesn't accept what she doesn't
fucking want.

Lillies

I dreamt of homo sapiens corpses fertilizing
lilium bolanderi beneath bonsai juniper trees
and breezes rattling snow white skin and bone of
blood red
bottom lip biting
breccia blondes
and all the while the sky-blue sky remains
sky-blue
and one plus one still equals two-
the last we knew
and you still love
I still love you
frankly, I'm not indubitably qualified to be a lily
yet anyways.

Cosmogyral Grief

It's Murphy's law in motion.
What can go wrong, has.
How do you come to terms in the face of death.
I've never been so petrified of the unknown.
watching his body simulate a decaying universe.
Every molecule of his 3rd dimensional body is
bursting with energy of impending release.
He's a star ready to burst,
He'll be my favorite supernova.

(In loving memory of David Carroll)

Philocalist Intimacy

As you lay yourself down to sleep,
I pray these words you will keep
riddles of verse and rhyme
conveying images Lichtenberg-burned
etched in my mind
serendipitous serenading sun and moon
eclipsed passing and knowing the unknown is
known unknowingly
And that mechanisms of domiciling become
disengaged
and disenchantment evolves to me enamored
waltzing in enchanted midnight forest
like your eyes, midnight at twilight forest
mystery
Mariana's trench deep
actually

to know what hearts there may scattered be on
ocean beds
and what dreams christen our heads

And what allegories to be told
the ebbing flow of motion
body, mind, soul
where yin acquaints with yang
quite literally the emboldened embodiments of
their being
To be discerned, to be discovered, or maybe
remembered.
take from that what you may
but as to slumber, you lay
you muse structure to my poetry
and she's the most profound facet of me
and maybe
the intrinsic nature of the words you can't yet
bring to light
and that's okay
I bid you a goodnight

Golden Gate Dissociation

Haight and Ashbury feels like a dream.
Was it yesterday or 2 years ago? I can't
remember.
I'm abundantly blessed and gratefully so,
although I'm seemingly dissociated from it all
now, often.
How I wish to be a whimsically bloomed
Alabama dandelion or fluttering California
monarch.
steps taken towards redemption resembling a
Salvador Dalian piece of work- contoured and
strange- a semblance of purpose to be found, yet
not understood.

I'm coming for you, zendom.

Obsessive Compulsive Boredom

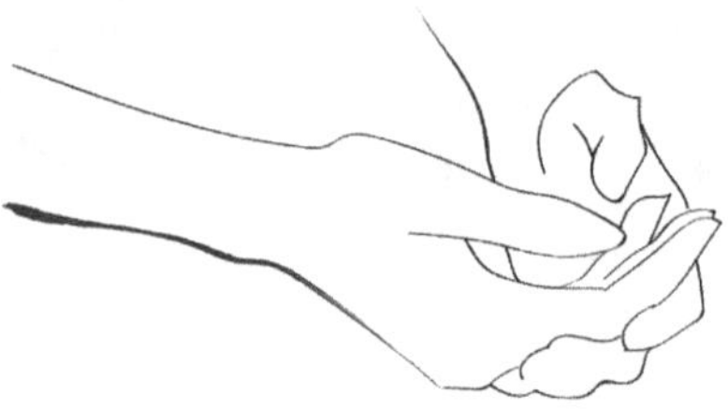

Bromidic winds whirl 'round boundless mind of mine.

mine fields in mind of mine checkering and crop circling and murderers to be

taut and

taunted and

taught.

And learned

And repeated

Academia too

Profanity and breadsticks, whatever.

Unexceptional, nondescript persons

Non denominational cults, what?

Bedridden ocean. Desire.

Fertilization in Lilliputian museums

Dust and dead skin

Really, I'm uninspired.

Moonlight and Mirrors

Sweet lunar love perched high on obsidian throne...

Perchance she quarrels with sun for reverence

Perchance she's intertwined in a perpetual and infinite cosmic waltz of duality

Perchance she became exasperated by the darkness, she chose to absorb Sun's radiancy

or

perchance she can never abscond
cimmerian truth and chose to reflect the light so
that others may not endure the blinding
emptiness of blistered blackness.

All I know for certain is that we innately
appreciate her presence and never once scorn her
for battles remnants marring her delicate surface.

do you see yourself in her the way i do?

Los Angeles Activism

Rain and champagne

Or was it

Ramen and sake

I'm unsure

but we were saving the world on state and
Victoria

We were, right?

Perhaps aimlessness and meanderings

Cherry lips at the Grenada

Star studded streets

Star studded skies

Presumably emaciated children only are

concerned with the latter

or neither

and the former ignores themselves and the skies
and the children

and innocence

but, reader, cherry lips are loud and sweet

and cherry lips kiss the sky and philosophers'
feet

Cherry lips

lunar eclipse

Festivals

And vestibules

Rituals

I mean

We're saving the world

We are, right?

Momentary Nihilsm

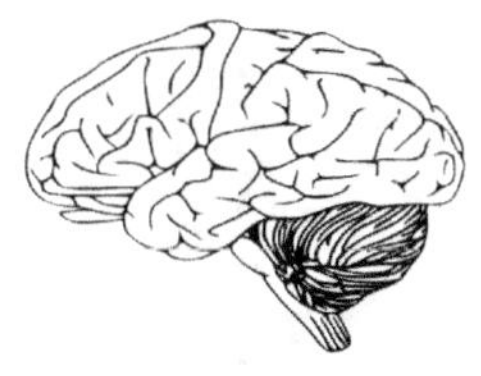

Onyx bullets screaming, ripping through
crystallized cerebral corridors

you are alone.

In mind

Body

Soul

in the world

you are alone.

Fractals of Creation

Who can debate his own requitance upon
acquisition of deliberated farces and far cries.

When the paintings resurrect-resuscitate
their very creators, and their creators force a
thunderstorm upon your orphic ocular orifices
and all the orphans of this world begin to cry.

Simultaneous redundancy.

There's never a victor in games for two.

Neither for the hauntress, written letters adorned
with pearls, lacquer, and love- never to be sent

Time to never be spent.

But synoptic plagiarizing Buddha said "hakuna
matata" or something like that,

This life doesn't exist anyways

but fuck the personified demagogues and
demigods- our love is real to us, our pain is real
to us.

But, honestly, who can debate his own
requitance?

Perpetual Returns Pen and Paper

Such a typical poet..
not reliable like the sun.
won't set and rise with predictably over the
Grecian coast.
We explode, send our bright bleeding colors
infinitely in all directions

Then just disappear only to come back in
glorious formation

Eventually...

Kind of like now

Like how

Words spun hurricanes upon my cerebellum

All the way to Russia and Iraq

and back.

But, as we are

to only pen some simple something in a
mediocre Athens cafe at 2 a.m

Welcome back.

Black, White, and Grey

There are days when even the sun himself
couldn't make me feel dim or diminished
in where i am SO sure of my path, passion,
place...person.
no map necessary — I know damn well who I
am and where I'm going in this painful world.
I'm going somewhere beautiful

Somewhere enchanted

Somewhere sacred

Somewhere home

I'm just so fucking sure of it..

The ethereal days of white-hot strength, intense
survivor-hood, unrepentant confidence

And although ephemeral, I'm just so damn
certain that those days, juxtaposed to the
darkness make that darkness livable

Until I get there

To the darkness

Until I'm laying at the bottom of my own
custom hell

The bottom of the 6 foot grave in the cemetery
of innocence, buried under the body weight of
every lonely man that bestowed upon me
another jewel in the crown of bloodied
memories on my toned-perfect blonde head.

Those days where the moon herself couldn't
make me feel anymore god damn small or pale

nor could she convince me that her marred,
scarred surface could compare to mine or her
dark side to be any closer to absolute zero than

the frigidness that has made home and hearth in
my very bones

Days when, no map could possibly even point
me in the right direction because I can't see
straight anyways, I can hardly breath without
choking on the "I'm fine-s" burning like the
poison whiskey those 2 words are

Days when I try to find a home in every eye that
i meet because..

Really..

I just need somewhere to rest my head

just for a minute

Just so I don't need to say "I'm. Fine."

one more fucking time or I'm pretty sure the fire
of those lies are going to engulf my entire being

I swear it

Like, I just want to sleep- you know?

It's hectic in there. The dreams and nightmares,
but at least they're not real, and that's the
coveted, sought after knowing

and then there's the in-between

and it might be the worst

Because it's just categorical nothingness

No shades of blue or of yellow

No light no dark

Just empty

Empty

Hollowed, taxidermic, paralyzing

empty

Empty like the space between the string and
quarks of atoms

Empty like both the cold and the warmth can't
find me

No map in the entire multiverse can help you...

or me find myself

inefficiency And

Ineffable vacancy

Absolute abyss

The days where I'm not the person or the
conversation

I am the pregnant pauses and lull between two
people conversing

not the pen or paper, but the space right before
they meet and create

anything at all

no achievements, no trauma

no likes, dislikes, fears, or favorites

an utter stillness in a mid-August golden hour

The days where even an entire universe...

Hell, even a forsaken city couldn't make me feel like I even exist.

The whirlwind world makes me dizzy.

It the Synecdoche

It's like having trilobites of information and knowing nothing.

It's like violently floating downward- to the molten core of Earth or falling upwards at a fiery heaven.

Or

It's having no gravity, yet being planted to the ground by the weight of your own fury, but drifting away because of the lightness of your hope.

It's being on fire while you drown in an oceanic landscape.

It's having poetry but no coherency

It's being weak but you're strong

It's having peace in the chaos

It's breathing while you suffocate

It's something about the yin yang effect.

It is everything that it isn't and isn't everything that it is -- without a definitive definition of "it. "

Crepuscular Betrayal

Morbid astrology

For

Agonizing anthology

And

Nonsensical

Analogy

Thank you for the cauldron

Black magic magistrate

Thank you for weaving together fibers and
shreds of hidden voodoo dolls once thought
demolished..

all with my face and my name

Graveyard craftsman

Thank you for pulling the trigger on every god
damn revolver and semiautomatic

that never had the safety on

 reserved to combat those around me

but not to be used on me

Master marksman

Thank you for painting my finally lilac

-most of the time- dreams

with blood and fear and shadows

again

again

again

Achillean artist

Thank you for plucking finally blossoming

Flowers from the infancy of my garden

Thank you for reverting my body back into a
crime scene

My favorite thing always was being bludgeoned
with knives called judgement being beheaded by
shameless guillotines called lack of control

Lobotomized by orbitoclasts called "maybe you
shouldn't have been there's"

And ripped open by gynecologic forceps named
"maybe you did or said something that could've
been construed as consent"

or "you just have to be more carefuls"

My favorite color was always shades of self
loathing and trauma

How'd you know?

Could you smell the minute innocence left on
me?

How could you tell that my favorite friends are
always the ones I'll always isolate from- when I
remember that my favorite taste has always been
the one cocktail of bitter regret, "it's my fault"s,
and a hungry man's sweat on my face

How did you realize my favorite position is the
one where I'm rendered immobilized powerless
and you wreck my body?

What gave it away?

How'd you figure out that I like to keep my soul
where I can't find it?

Like right now.

Thank you for reminding me of who I was built
to be.

Fresh linen blue candles aren't for girls like me

Floral arrangements in bright springtime
mornings aren't for girls like me

Decadent tastes and savory spices aren't for girls
like me

The feeling of dewy grass blades under
subtropic Costa Rican rainbows aren't for girls
like me

Girls like me ask for it, right?

Girls like me should've had better boundaries,
right?

Girls like me shouldn't have hourglass bodies or
our time wouldn't be stolen by scavengers in the
night, right?

Girls like me deserve our demons

Deserve our pain

To be, within our own selves, an outsider.

Thanks for the reminder.

Metanoia

and I've always entrusted myself to the promises
of my dreams.

and I've always braced for those moments when
I'm blatantly reminded why..

and such as now, I'm captive to precognitive
truth aren't I?

And how I knew your gentle kisses, only
surpassed by the beating and benevolence of
your heart,

before i really knew

and how i could taste your valor, burning,
passing through my lips

and strength, as if you've held the weight of the
world, before you ever lifted me

and how that makes me steadfast to conquer and
to keep

and how i wanted to tell you that i Fucking love
you at least a dozen times

and how we were sitting on the same beach that
this fire was conjured to life

and that day the sky was on fire too, but it
couldn't possibly have been burning brighter or
more apparent than the words that came from
my soul, but stuck in my throat as razors

and how we left our secrets under the light of 14
trillion stars, swirling in the element of our
existences.

and how i was laying there reading Rumi in my
mind

and he said "Your task is not to seek for love,
but merely to seek and find all the barriers
within yourself that you have built against it."

and i caught a glimpse of opportunity to listen...
for once

and how i did

and how i committed to continue

and how i feel as entire seas are ebbing and
flowing violently with grandeur and life and
they flow inside of me

and how i used to think this place was the
destination, yet now to see it's only the
beginning

that the moon only shines brighter the more that
you should climb to her

and how you are in a field of basking golden
sunflowers that are me

And the purple black past is repudiated by the
antiquated tastes of 100 tomorrows

and i'm there too.

Intimacy

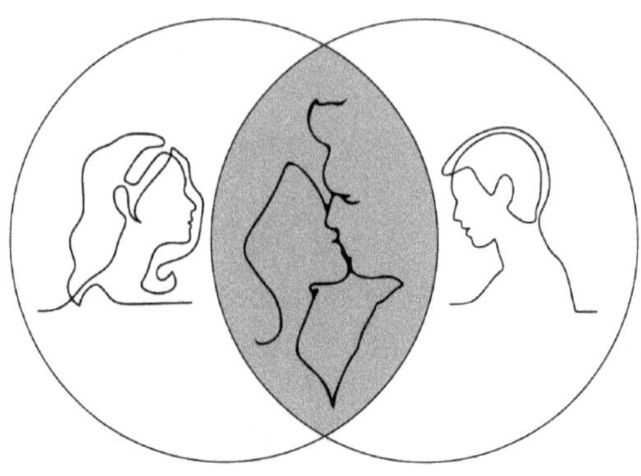

witching hours beseeched two.

consummation and conscious

cosmos coursing through crevices and
hemoglobin corridors.

The Jamaican's clavinet exaggerating neck
kisses from hearts of dying stars-- and of you,
sweet lover.

Bongos riveting, revival of tempo, dictation of
our rhythmic rivers, blissful fornication.

Two to become one without diminution of one

because principa Mathematica is theoretic

and my body was an alter

revered, honored, commemorated

Surely he repented there, and part of him was irrecoverably

entranced

lost

kept there.